BLACK APPLES

enlarged second edition

POEMS BY LYN LIFSHIN

a crossing press book

Acknowledgments:

Books: *Why Is The House Dissolving? (Open Skull Press, 1968)
Leaves and Night Things (Baby John Press, 1970)*

Periodicals: *Abraxas, Aldebaran Review, Arx, Cafe Solo,
Carolina Quarterly, December, Epos, Folio, Gnosis, Greenfield
Review, Hanging Loose, Hearse, The Lit, Lung Socket, New:
American & Canadian Poetry, South Florida Poetry Journal,
Wisconsin Review, Wormwood.*

Graphics by David Sykes

SBN: 0-912278-30-7

TABLE OF CONTENTS

INTRODUCTION

This second, enlarged edition of *Black Apples* contains 13 more poems from two earlier chapbooks: *Why Is The House Dissolving?* (Open Skull Press) and *Leaves and Night Things* (Baby John Press). In essence this edition presents the best of Lyn Lifshin's work from its beginnings up through 1970.

Lyn Lifshin is, 1st. of all, a lyricist; like a true lyricist she moves words around with endless invention and variation to achieve her effects. These effects are dependent not so much on a philosophy or on a use of metaphor or rhetoric as they are on a sense of phrasing and breath. Where an Elizabethan lyricist, for instance, would use the pastoral convention for his counters and traditional verse for his form, Lyn Lifshin uses today's sexual revolution as her convention and a subtle, molten (almost breathless) phrasing for her open forms. What you get in her poetry are dramatically-breathed lyrics that document men/women sexual relationships in great variety and freshness. She can be alternately tender, tough, helpless, or joyous depending on her mood.

She writes good bawdy poems as well--verse that makes you grin or marvel at what she can suggest (read "Chewing Up the Sun," "In Spite of His Dangling Pronoun," and "Nice"). Her range dows not stop here: she not only understands love, sex, and bawdy but she writes about her living, mythic past--the world of immigrant aunts, uncles, parents who were "seadreamt from Lithuania" and who ended up in the snowy hills of Vermont cut off from their old-world culture and finding, or losing, their way in a new.

And this new world is full of perils for the materially possessed, sexually repressed who live here. Lyn Lifshin understands what it means to live in a so-called "free society." Read "Why is The House Dissolving?" and that devastating poem of middle-class marriage, "The Way Sun Keeps Falling Away from Every Window."

The poems in this collection are blunt and strong medicine; *Black Apples* is a major work by a rare poet.

John Gill
Trumansburg, N.Y.

BUT INSTEAD HAS GONE INTO WOODS

A girl goes into the woods
and for what reason
disappears behind branches
and is never heard from again.
We don't really know why
she could have gone shopping
or had lunch with her mother
but instead has gone into
woods, alone, without the lover
and not for leaves or flowers.
It was a clear bright day
very much like today.
It was today. Now you might
imagine I'm that girl, it
seems there are reasons. But
first consider I don't live
very near those trees and my
head is already wild with branches.

WHY IS THE HOUSE DISSOLVING?

Roses are covered like
coffins though it is still
rather warm and neighbors
wonder should they plant identical
hedges, put the same screens on
windows of their very similar heads?
And now part of their ritual, the
daily painting of houses, each day
a different color as if they wanted
to change they spray the windows put up
doors and hose the pool and
sweep garages.
But see that strange hole
in the limb of the oldest tree
sucking everything up, how everything
dries, is shriveling inside it?
Yes, this is our house but it's hard to
remember, do we really live here?
We have doors and garages but
where are we growing, where
are our windows, have we any real shelter?
And why, so slowly we can hardly see it,
is the house dissolving very very softly, being
swallowed up in the bark of the old
                                    screaming branches?

COLORS THAT ARE PEELING AWAY

Arms and legs grow
under the sound but
love is pulling away
from their bodies,
something cuts across
everything they can
ever know. As if to
suck the dark out of
his hands her breasts
fall into new orbits,
nipples stretching
higher than leaves or
mountains, new avalanches
unfolding in her thighs.
But the sand still pushes
into their foreheads, colors
peal off everything they try to
hold. All their rooms keep breaking.
A city of leaves
starts to grow inside her muscles
but when she tries to reach him
the leaves turn into old photographs
and she is running in them
falling, smaller, dissolving
somewhere along the lost grass of
a super four lane highway thru his heart.

SHE SIGH HAPPY

She going to town
legs shaved way up
to see if he knocked her
up doctor say press legs apart
on the table with white towel
covering cunt, metal prong scratching
inside slit   cold she think
and he pressing her belly,
then looking at juice
he says not to worry.
And as she trots home
blood warmly in her nylon crotch
she sigh happy
red shining sticky down her leg.

NOT QUITE SPRING

Baby you know I get high
on you, come back with me
whispering in her ear
it was all she could do to say
no, spring leaves budding,
his hand on her breast
crocus smell and
everything unfolding
she gasping I want, I
would but instead hurrying
back to the windowless room
where she locks the heavy door.
Lemons are rotting on her pillow,
she studies her nipples,
nyloned crotch in mirror
then hugs her huge body to sleep.

CHEWING UP THE SUN

She had been really
looking for some
plumber -- being 23 and
only tapped about
the edges   and when she
saw his pink tipped
plunger thickly flaring
from a swollen bag she felt
that he could probably
please her. so when he
came to diddle in her
toilet she locked
him snug in her dark
spongy hamper
gobbled down the rusty
key then raised her
lid to show him
what she had and what
she wanted. and he climbed
inside her
medicine cabinet   pushed
aside her toothpaste
knees her fluffy
bathmat   ripping tiles
from all her corners while
he probed her bowl's
strange gulping
noises till water screamed

out of their drains. and
he stayed inside her
rubbery places and
he came and plunged and
came and hardly anyone
noticed how
they lived among sweet
towels and talcum   never
taking time to
shave   how his tools were
always ready   how her
ducts had softly
changed   or heard sounds of
joy and dampness
spilling wild from the
hot misty room
as their bodies reached out
to chew up the sun

THE WAY SUN KEEPS FALLING AWAY FROM EVERY WINDOW

This is the kind
of marriage they live in:
split and stuffed with
terrible dead furniture,
he doing anything he
can to make her
happy, saving up a
big stiff
bankroll while she drowns
in hills of carpet
wanting what she doesn't
know he's going to buy
automatic brooms
for poking
deep in all her
corners, machines to make her
panties whirl at varied
speeds and circles, bouncing
but it all stays
wrong   it isn't what
either of them wanted. Take me she wants
to scream, even on the
staircase, even in the daylight
nuzzle down my stomach
with all your tongues   but
instead she talks of oranges and lettuce
and mornings orders
rape from the milkman, boxes
thick with cream and fears each night that time of

grey teeth, that her nipples
suddenly fall like wrinkled lemons, dreams
a parade of hair and cocks, hot scrotum marching
grinding against her
in through her flannel crotch,
wild in her
vagina --- balls like wet suns muscling her
flesh, great mounds of dampness, the
dream exploding birds
in all her mouths   her teeth are clogged with
sperm and feathers
and she wakes, longing, startled,
her lips pressed thin,
wondering of stains they could leave,
                    a smell of something
that is animal.
But the sheets are dryer than leaves
nothing has been
touched, the hair between their thighs stays smooth,
unruffled.
Sun falls away from every window
and a noise keeps biting under the meat of her eyes,
her throat wants something more than
glass and linen.
In closets of shoes and old guitars she
waits, is touching where he never
enters, falls lost among the lonely shoes and
                    rusty dresses,
waiting, but almost certain that they can
                    never really come to be together.

NEW ENGLAND SEA NIGHT OF SNOW
LIPS, VISIONS

A skinny moon that is hardly.
The snow ragged swamp trees.

Bones of remembered faces
are blown white in winter
alphabets. Snow lips

Cranberry lips. A vision of
sailors' lips knocking at

sea rock and stubble.
And the coldest sea ever.

Fish wreathed in ice
gleam. Are stars, salt stars.

Are whiter than snow gulls.
And miraculous turtles

bloom in dreams of the
high school science teacher.

He sees them circling a
summer moon of warm leaves
and not his own death for once,

tho New England dark stings,
the wind full of so many

night horses and no riders

REASONS FOR STAYING

There were
floods
      o don't go
      back   nothing's
      the same
the roads are
gone your
heavy girl
was under water
20 days she's
all white
and bloated

But no there wasn't
a famine
      all the
      fish washed up
      in her
      face
           she's even
           fatter

has gills and
thick scales

don't go back

THEY ARE SINGING PSALMS

All the lamps have
shades of plastic

the wouldbe barefoot children
are wearing other people's shoes.

Hush, they are singing psalms
banishing odors from human bodies

and everyone is drowning
in plush pile gold carpet

OVER AND OVER

in july
moths camped in her
clothes

later he paid all the
bills and when

winter came
had a new
depressing relationship

which he paints
over and over

waving purple
goodbyes from the mad
house window

FOR AN OCTOPUS

You, baby who left a
broad with chocolate eyes
and enormous tits to come
stumbling out of the West
with broken shoes and a
vision of Jewish hair and
thighs to this place so
full of leaves and dresses,
didn't you know I hoarded
boozing poets, stole their
words and dreamed impossible
flesh picnics and even love
for a sun week maybe   but
never that you'd come to
stay this long. And now
having you around all the
time waving tentacles and
moaning, it's true I've
wanted you back in the clock
some days: with all your
moods and wanting me to
cry when you cry, it's not
what I expected you know.
Usually, it's better

LEANING OVER THE BRIDGE
AT OTTER CREEK

February after rain
the rocks lizard grey
lean against the stone

raw wind touches
taste the sounds of
new roots coming
even this early

stand and watch
winter dripping slow
from the gargoyles
branches in the whirlpool

look for something
of that strange girl
who leaped into the
breaking up snow

that distant spring
when faces sneered
the water pulled her

watch for her shadow
to come floating
high over the chestnut
trees and the church

spire blurred in the
distance. Listen
for March to
break in the water

DREAM OF BLACK APPLES, WAR

Four people are
encased in a coach
that's going to be burned.
I don't know if it's relevant.
Am I one of the four?

When we wake up
some people are talking of war.
This must be the space before it happens.
The apples are frozen black by morning

You think shots
ring out nearby.
Later the wind swells everywhere,
hurling us toward something.
By noon the bedroom is full of strangers

You are still gentle
but never seem to want me lately
altho I'm not sure,
with all these other people

For the first time now
we are sealing the windows
as if that could shut out the fear.
Why is it, especially now, I want your thighs
knit inside me? I'm afraid,

I wish the house would take root.
But the rooms tremble
doors blast off and dissolve
I can't find you

And for once don't think how
I seem to the others,
taking off my shoes to run
barefoot on stones where the floor was

carrying a package of ruined clothes
I don't know where

AFTER WHAT THE NEWS IS

numbers in our heads.
a map of broken trees
but no faces.

small spoons of death
scrape against us and
tunnel in thru the wood of
our houses,
gasping

NEVER THE CITY'S NAME

Coming early spring
with winter buds still frozen,
seadreamt from Lithuania,

the nine brothers and sisters
and your ten thin years and cold
Boston early March, the weather

just turning. But no words for
telling then. What were the other
reasons later when I was coloring the

crossing--were you skimming the
water sleekly on a walrus or floating in
on a pink gull, puffing like a fat man

or on a dove's wing
flying over all the houses?
I used to wonder but you never said,

maybe remembering a place you left but
never telling except that there were
feather beds and ducks and chickens in the

distant house, tremendous pines.
But all the years we shared the same rooms
as if together,

you never gave the city's name
or yourself.

CEREMONY

All day they
bring the face
breaking open

The man who was murdered
spills against us,
an assassin still at large
across the screen

We unpack suitcases
anyway, never
not listening.
Loss keeps getting undressed
before our eyes

And microphone cables
catch in the reporters'
flesh like a
web of sea growth

dragging them
past cameras toward a
darkness of their
own tho
they appear to be
listing figures and
arrangements
calmly

tho their faces seem
with us,
comforting our air

with words
for the body falling over
and over

As if those linked in this
glow of pain
could never be alone

FAMILY

my grandfather
in a jar of herring
waiting in back of the
movies, his
mustache full of dill

checked things
out in the
52 Plymouth he
drove to Saratoga
long after he was 80

his yellow leer
for holy days
and ladies

confided his
regrets

mostly to the
redmaple wind

BERYL

My father in his
sister's dark house
chanting like a
Jew. Candles,
Friday wine

Everything there had a
peculiar heavy
richness
flushed cheeks and
velvet, amber shawls.
A fat smell of praying

In Vermont in
rooms plain grey and
wooden
I remember his sitting
those nights without
a word and
how he stood in the park,
listened to chestnuts dropping.
But not much else

only just now
I'm saying
Beryl, his
sleek Hebrew name,
I didn't even know
I knew it

Is that what he
wanted back

or what?

FAMILY 8

Another uncle
was a pathological liar
but so gentle with whores,

bringing them dogs and flowers.
Law school then a cluttered
five to dime, mainly toys and
needles but under the counter

squirting from split knees,
maiden juice it said,
just press the button.

Twelve years of Sundays
were always with the Irish girl
but secretly, that her iceblue eyes
the family shouldn't see, and

slow afternoons in the rented room
till at fifty love grew thin
so he married the rabbi's daughter,
but he never had a son.

WAITING, THE HALLWAYS UNDER
HER SKIN THICK WITH DREAMCHILDREN

Lace grows in her eyes like
fat weddings,
she is pretty, has been baking

bisquits of linen to stuff into his mouth
all her life,

waiting for him. The hallways
under her skin are thick with dreamchildren.

Who he is hardly matters, her rooms
stay for him,

her body crying to be taken
with rings and furniture, tight behind doors

in a wave of green breath and wild rhythm,
in a bed of
lost birds and feathers,

smiling, dying

THE VISIT

Each time we come there are a few extra stairs.

We want to be tired when we get there and
sleep in the dark orchid room.

Insects eat through screens,
the closet is full of dead clothes

and David's letters.

In the morning we eat as much as we can and
talk of wars and parties, the new prints we bought
were they expensive?

Will they last?

Say something to please or to
make people laugh. Don't hurt anyone or explain.

But why does my sister stay locked
in a strange rage, alone, behind closed doors?

Bad paintings on the walls, the wood is
being eaten away

and those old plastic flowers.

Still an apple tree grows outside the apartment window
where no tree should,
tall and thin with very small green apples.

Later we go to the new shop
that was once a First National
and throw nails down over the abandoned railroad,

walk past the brick town house and
all the clapboard homes where daughters of Episcopal
ministers used to live.

Back in the high rooms
there are photographs of relatives
newly dead. A father, my father I think,
pasted on mirrors

from 1938 or 39.

And the waterfall rushes, even in
July, the creek waters in the orchid room are

louder than crying.

We must sort things out, talk about stocks and settlements,
the divorce that was stopped by his death.

Night beetles fall upsidedown to the floor
near dusty bottles.

Later in the day we leave, put the heavy love at a distance.
These images can never be unified

or undone

THAW

Ice comes undone
Skin shining and
hair full of
March

girls spill out of
offices their
bones whispering strong
hands to marry

glazed orchards
and vines coming back
Green is under the
snow the girls'

arms seem to open
as if to lift them past
fluorescent air
toward whatever

mysteries
are hidden from them
Later nearly
blinded by water and

light they'll
move a 1 o'clock wave
their hair folding
back into

rooms of
machines and paper   But
no desks can
hold such

dreaming blood,
drunk on the poems
sun makes
in their bodies

TWO SNOW AND RUST SUNDAYS

Snow, the color of
rust and wind that
scrapes the old
railroad ties

No trains
anymore, just
Sunday bells
they knock the grey
sky, smoke falling

Close to this
blurred hill
whispered and now
mostly forgotten,

Patty Bissette
strangled in Boston
that winter, a
different Sunday

gone in a scream
of blood stockings

(and whose baby
in her the
town kept wondering)

Snow and rust bless her

I lived here once too

YOU UNDERSTAND THE REQUIREMENTS

We are
sorry to have to
regret to
tell you
sorry sorry
regret sorry that you have
failed

your hair should have been
piled up higher

you have failed to
pass failed
your sorry
regret your
final hair comprehensive
exam satisfactorily
you understand the requirements

you understand we are
sorry final

and didn't look as professional
as desirable
or sorry dignified
and have little enough
sympathy for 16th century
sorry english anglicanism

we don't know doctoral
competency what to think and
regret you will sorry not
be able to stay
or finish

final regret your disappointment
the unsuccessfully completed best
wishes for the future
it has been a
regret sorry the requirements
the university policy

please don't call us.

IN SPITE OF HIS DANGLING PRONOUN

He was really her favorite
student dark and just
back from the army with
hot olive eyes, telling her of
bars and the first
time he got a piece of
ass in Greece or was it
Italy and drunk on some strange
wine and she thought
in spite of his dangling
pronoun (being twenty four and
never screwed but in her
soft nougat thighs) that he
would be a
lovely experience.
So she shaved her legs up high
and when he came
talking of footnotes she
locked him tight in her
snug black file cabinet where
she fed him twice a day and
hardly anyone noticed
how they lived among bluebooks
in the windowless office
rarely coming up for sun or the
change in his pronoun or the
rusty creaking chair
or that many years later
they were still going to town in
novels she never had time to finish

IN THAT HOUSE

a film grows over
everything near them.

They want to
outlaw leaves, clasp

armour over wrists
and fingers.

Air catches in
rooms full of no,

even when they
sleep their blood

keeps drowning.
Just watch how their

children tremble
trying to run in tight

shoes of glass
and falling

ICE MOVING
THRU NIGHT WINDOWS OF BLOOD

Paint the windows
shut but
it's no use
ice comes inside
fills those
holes in me. What
kind of a
life is this
getting up at
3 AM,
feeling up the
night for
someone to
touch.
What kind of a
woman is it
wants a
warmth
in that close,
puts wire
around her
self you
can't
get in there

TO BE STRUCK ALIVE
BY DIFFERENT WEATHER

Dawn spills out of
slate sky. But it's a dawn of moldy words, old

fingers: colors of knives and concrete.
My skin waits

for an orangejuice sun, to be struck alive by
different weather.

Still the room drowns. He said, Baby you'd better
choose now.

Beating, beating. Under the mountain of grey
sheets, no answer.

Verbs of dust
hurt my eye. But I don't see how to

go with him.
Or how to stay in these walls I can't live in

where everything
falls with the frost-brown apples, where an

icebird keeps
banging against the window. And cries for what is

green and warm
keep bruising the glass inside my bones.

HOW IT HAPPENED

Even there
we were drawing past
one another. Even in the same city
we fell sideways, were
lips that kept
getting to places a little too early

or late. Of course, it wasn't really that
dramatic. But the way
letters were banging at rooms
where no one was living,
and your name in the phonebooks still seeming
magical. At least, real. A small mystery to eat me.

Now I have to laugh,
the way I thought that what went wrong
was geographic.
Put it this way: these crazy voices
scheme a star in the middle of
checkbooks and marriage. They glue it up with bluewood

and letters and arms and then sleep with it
tightly, move into it as deep as they can.
They go blind.
And never understand how it happened.
Or that it is already dissolving. Shadows in direct
light. Dreams. But you know that story.

SOMEDAY

Someday you will find
your possessions are not what they seemed
A penis will sprout
out of the bathtub drain,
the chairs growing roots
deep into carpets. Thin translucent men
will hide slyly in your furnace,
you won't be able to get them to leave
sing as many groundhog carols as you choose.
At almost the same time
worms will be sprouting from your piano
and a very large nose will come and
steal your cantaloupe at breakfast.
Isn't this awful you'll want to cry as
wool is melting to blood on your skin.
But even if you scream nobody will notice.
Could you, truthfully, expect anyone to believe it?

POEM FOR THE HOUSE
BEING EATEN BY WATER

The whole house
slants to the lake
water coming
deep on one side
up to your knees and
purple ivy
on the other
Not much else but
bleached wood
Julie and
Rod cut
into a grey board
fuck on another
Two brothers lived here
till 1939
each in a quiet
locked room
with no
friends
If you come over
anytime, just
don't leave
by the
back door

I DON'T WANT YOUR BLACK
RIDING MY BONES

You take those
black hairs
of your heart,

I don't need them.

your darkness
riding my
bones

climbs stairs
in me

3 at a time.

I don't have to
keep balling midnight

PULLING OUT

First their eyes
pull toward new underwater
places, a terrible dark
gill catching her attention,

she didn't know he was like this,
heart scooped, full of glassware and
tin. But she still wants him
breathing in her

body, grows new lips and muscles, gold
mirrors in her side until he
moans that he can't stand
her spying. And their mouths fill with

stones. But they go on
anyway in this water that keeps
everything slow, his metal
penis still moving in her, the holes

in her side leak so slowly
it's hard to tell what's
lost. Only, they're
having this trouble, the floor slides

away, they can't tell where they
stand, her thighs won't
hold him. Words
come heavy too and hang

like blood sealed in plastic. Love
is certainly pealing away
and all she wanted
was something warm, green

water to flow inside her body,
smoke her heart.
But he slips from the places she dreamed
he would know, her gills are so

lonely --- yes it's just like
any movie   run it
backwards see the lips pull out, bodies
twisting upright.

Arms float without any direction.
Salt comes and it's
all shell and separation,
love jerking down their throats, hooks

and weeds taking them, spreading in
their hair. All their reflections
breaking.   Torn pieces of
her glass scrape his metal   she

misses his bones but
they're both bloated from being in this
water too long
                    o let's get out of

here she cries couldn't
we live in a
mountain   in a glacier on a green
stone somewhere

but something in them has been turning
so hard   clots of coral
loss so brittle
that they break, and splinter

so raggedly
nobody can touch them

EATING THE RAIN UP

        grey tuesday
rain all
night
you said do you
        want to go
                for cigarettes
                        do you want to

                    listen
        i've got a
        room we
                could
i've got something i want
you
        at least
we could
        talk

                tell me your name

books fell across the bed
your mustache
                was the kind, i
            wrapped your mouth
        into me
                yes i knew
            your thighs would be
            friendly, your
hair closing
        down
                small hands a pillow

                and the
            wetness we grasped
        that warm together

                    ate the rain up

ON ANOTHER COAST

Maybe
could it have
been because of
rain that we fell
together so
easily that first time
rain keeping the
others near the
fire your hair was
blacker than the melon
seeds under the straw the towels
smelling of sweet trees our
bodies lifted to each other in the
rain cottage the
wet leaves pulling us
close and down

LIGHT FROM THIS TURNING

I have lost touch with
distant trees,
the wind you brought
in your hair
and lilac hills.

Something different
bites into the river
and the river of lost days
floats over my tongue.

Love, you are like that
distant water, pulling
and twisting,
you turn me

apart from myself
like some frightening road,
something I don't want
to know.

Still, let my
hair float slow through
this new color,
let my eyes absorb
all light

from this turning
that has brought us
here, has carried us
to where we are,
we are

TO POEM

all night
you banged
in my head
poking your fingers
thru me, hot for
blood and then
in the morning
stretching out on
the table
flaunting your muscles
when you knew there wasn't time.
Later in the car
you made me dizzy.
but worse, how you
made my love jealous
perching in my hair
with those stiff wings.
and now, bastard
alone with me finally
the chance to
scares you off

I'D LIKE TO LIVE HERE
A WHILE IT'S ALL

so open   the house
floats to the lake
sun lights up the webs
i'd wait for the
leaves to grow close
water make love to my
thighs
        good not to have
to think of walls and
bodies the cracked glass
shining like a lake
too and weeds thru the
floor
        i could forget
i ever wanted to be
your lady, letting the
rusty wind in, listening
to nothing

EVEN THERE

it was December
and yes finally
you wanted me
we ran down the
slick narrow road
houses leaned
together the colors
wine and brown
remember the cracked
snow our scarves
floating getting
there out of
breath our
hair melting
boots clicked under
the door there
were quilts on the
sloped ceiling
and the old
stove you smiled
toward going to
heat up some
coffee. I kept
looking around
to get it right:
your suede jacket
hanging in several
places your
mouth was
corduroy I wanted
to touch
but even in the
dream every
time I came
close to you
the place that
was you
changed to air

LEMON WIND

All day
nobody wanted
to talk

the sleeping bags
were still wet
from the storm
in Cholla Vista

Nothing went right.

But later the
wood we
burned had a sweet
unfamiliar smell

and all night
we could taste
lemons in the wind

MUSTACHE

I was thinking
of it this
morning, those
marvelous hairs that
curl around your words

and how they smelled with
frost all over
in the mountains

And yes especially of that
time on the floor
looking like the
middle part of a thick
leggy bug I could

just see
above my belly, moist and
floating up
asked

is this
making your blood glow

ON THE NEW ROAD

red sumac presses
against the windshield,
tires moan

Your wife dreams
you are guilty,

I button and unbutton
what I feel

BRANCHES
AND THE WETNESS OF TREES

Waiting
in Ricky's small house,
the all day snow on branches
and the wetness of trees.

Frost
and your eyes of
slow fireplaces, a fire
on everything, the room darkly
bright and

you
said to
lie close,
it was
what we both wanted.

How it was
just this time of year,
winter in another town, locked
and colored over now as this

old glass snowflake ball,
turn it over, watch it snow again.

FOR A FRIEND

Leaving beer and apples
on the window
for later
lying together those nights
till four,
talking
everybody must have thought
that we were
lovers
your red mustache in the blanket
smell of your cigarette in my hair
white thighs in the mountains
getting bombed on the sky

But when I stand
back I don't recognize
myself or
you love
who got into my skirt
and blood
before I knew
your name and then
wanted to be
mostly friends

Those 3 weeks
everything that moved in my
bones stretched
toward you,

I wanted to take you inside me that deep
your crooked smile, Russian
eyes but you
grew into the desk, your
back a wall

What were
you feeling those
nights we undressed, then
in the dark
you asked who else I could
talk to like this
while I was wondering what to do
with feelings I
couldn't use,
your face
so close to mine
it chilled me

LUST BLOWING UNDER THE DOOR, BRIGHT AS STRAW

Your smile's like sun
flowers he said
as tho
embarrassed his
hands were
pressing
awkwardly the
ring on his
second finger
close to her
eyes
from that room
a wheat sea
lust
blew under the
door bright
as straw
and his warm
parts on
her belly
those small
bones that changed her
small
bones to water
And not even
knowing
his name
until later
when the floor fell
the room
turned into a
painting
and the paint cracked

HEAR THE BODIES GETTING LOUDER

This could be where the
story ends, if it
is a story.
Afternoon, their
lust played out
for certain,
they'd moaned love
and listen baby.
He gets drunk
and she doesn't even
notice, it's not the first
time. Now his voice
slurs across the table,
cracked words
fall down his clothes
and she turns,
escapes in her hair,
letting the green leaves he
hates close her off.
It's at a window over the sand
and she leans deeper
away, a stone listening for
water, letting the waves
crash. I am that
girl let's say and you, if you
are there might hear the
bodies getting louder and
louder, as tho
something inside was
near breaking
tho right now everything
is at the still
edge of a
scream

NICE

floating thru chairs
then opening
your hand
snakes in thru corduroy
my slip rides up the sun
makes the rug into a wool beach
sand   assapples   a wave of
thighs opening
skin prints a v on the rug your
knees go there
opening
and mouths suddenly too a
crack touch the pink smell
the sleek breathing flesh moans
a taste is nipples
bumping and your sail of blood
shove of bone tongue
travelling into this moist
lips opening the first bang of
hair and clothes rise from bodies
tremble the warm buttons rubbing
scratch of your mouth there
the damp nylon crotch
petals dissolving in a water my silk
hips you open and your fingers
under plunge so are pressing lips there
and your flesh
root shining

rocks your heat to my belly and my
legs spread so wide
greedy for the whole boat of you
in me your lovejuice dipping these
sloppy hills of cunt and you
put your good
hardness up me   opening
skin rooms pounding
and circles slide your raw stem
my nails pull you
tighter
in and the slap of licked flesh oil
waves lunging and teeth
that eat everywhere ramming
the slit wet
opening and spread so
wide and splitting bite the sweet hot ache swell
your bomb breaking
too sucks the whole room up
fur zippersbeercans
and the sweat hair of groaning and sperm
till your cock bud throbs more
to ball me over and
again   better than summer
deep and nice
bringing everything
home